# DWIGHT HOWARD
## Basketball Superstar

BY JOANNE MATTERN

CAPSTONE PRESS
a capstone imprint

Sports Illustrated KIDS Superstar Athletes is published by Capstone Press,
151 Good Counsel Drive, P.O. Box 669, Mankato, Minnesota 56002.
www.capstonepub.com

Library of Congress Cataloging-in-Publication Data
Mattern, Joanne, 1963–
  Dwight Howard : basketball superstar / by Joanne Mattern.
    p. cm.—(Sports illustrated kids, superstar athletes)
  Includes bibliographical references and index.
  Summary: "Presents the athletic biography of Dwight Howard, including his career
as a high school and professional basketball player"—Provided by publisher.
  ISBN 978-1-4296-6563-6 (library binding)
  ISBN 978-1-4296-7307-5 (paperback)
  1.  Howard, Dwight—Juvenile literature. 2.  Basketball players—United States—Biography—
Juvenile literature.  I. Title. II. Series.
  GV884.H68M38 2012
  796.323092—dc22
  [B]                                                          2011001023

**Editorial Credits**
Christopher L. Harbo, editor; Ted Williams, designer; Eric Gohl, media researcher;
    Eric Manske, production specialist

**Photo Credits**
Getty Images Inc./Doug Benc, 5; WireImage/Paul Abell, 9
Newscom/KRT Sports/Gary W. Green, 6
Sports Illustrated/Bill Frakes, 1, 7, 14, 21, 22 (top); Bob Rosato, cover (right), 2–3, 13, 17, 23;
    Damian Strohmeyer, 10; John Biever, 22 (bottom), 24; John W. McDonough, cover (left), 15, 18,
    22 (middle)

**Design Elements**
Shutterstock/chudo-yudo, designerpix, Fassver Anna, Fazakas Mihaly

**Direct Quotations**
Pages 11, 16 from January 26, 2005, *IGN Sports* interview with Dwight Howard by Victor
    Kelly, http://sports.ign.com

Printed in the United States of America in North Mankato, Minnesota.
032011        006110CGF11

# TABLE OF CONTENTS

# CHAPTER 1

# RECORD NIGHT

On November 15, 2005, the Orlando Magic faced the Charlotte Bobcats. The Magic's 19-year-old **center**, Dwight Howard, put on a show. In the first half, Howard scored 15 points. He also grabbed nine **rebounds**.

**center**—a basketball player who usually plays near the basket and is often the tallest player on the team
**rebound**—the act of gaining possession of the ball after a missed shot

Howard continued his attack in the second half. He scored another six points. He didn't let up on the **boards** either.

**board**—a rebound in basketball

By the end of the game Howard had a new record. He was the youngest player ever to score at least 20 points and grab 20 rebounds in one game.

# CHAPTER 2

# ATLANTA STAR

Dwight David Howard was born December 8, 1985. He grew up in Atlanta, Georgia. Sports were important to his family. His father was the athletic director at Southwest Atlanta Christian Academy. Both of his parents played college sports. Howard started playing basketball when he was 9 years old.

Howard played high school basketball for Southwest Atlanta Christian Academy. In four years he **averaged** more than 16 points and 13 rebounds per game. In his senior season, he won two National Player of the Year awards. Reporters called him the best high school player in the country.

**average**—to find the typical number of points scored or rebounds grabbed in each game

"I want to be the best player ever in my era."—Dwight Howard

# CHAPTER 3

# STRAIGHT TO THE PROS

Howard's hoops skills took him straight to the National Basketball Association (NBA). In 2004 the Orlando Magic picked him in the first round of the **draft**. In his first season, Howard averaged 12 points a game. He also became the youngest player to average at least 10 rebounds a game.

**draft**—the process of choosing a person to join a sports team

In 2005–2006 Howard learned to be a better **defender**. He had a career-high 26 rebounds in one game. By season's end he led the NBA with 1,022 rebounds. This total included 734 defensive rebounds.

**defender**—a player who tries to keep the other team from scoring

## MAGIC NUMBER

As a child, Howard was a huge fan of Kevin Garnett. When Garnett played for the Minnesota Timberwolves, he wore jersey number 21. To honor Garnett, Howard wears number 12 on his jersey. Howard's number is Garnett's old number reversed.

Howard had a fantastic 2006–2007 season. He averaged 17.6 points and 12.3 rebounds per game. The Magic reached the NBA playoffs. In 2007–2008 his numbers increased. He averaged 20.7 points and 14.2 rebounds per game. After the season, Howard helped the U.S. Olympic basketball team win a gold medal.

**"The NBA is not for everybody ... it seems so easy from just watching, but on the court it is a whole different level." —Dwight Howard**

In 2008–2009 the Magic reached the NBA Finals. The Los Angeles Lakers won. But Howard's playoff numbers were amazing. He scored 467 points and grabbed 353 rebounds in 23 games. In 2009–2010 Howard averaged 18.3 points and 13.2 rebounds per game. He helped the Magic return to the playoffs.

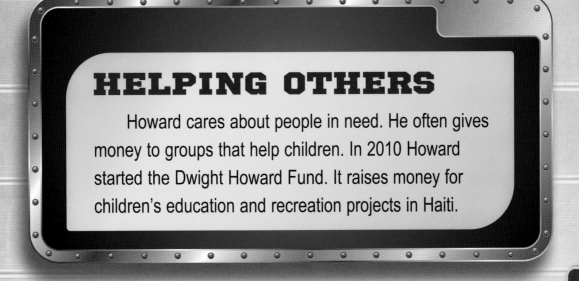

## HELPING OTHERS

Howard cares about people in need. He often gives money to groups that help children. In 2010 Howard started the Dwight Howard Fund. It raises money for children's education and recreation projects in Haiti.

# CHAPTER 4

# TEAM PLAYER

In just a few seasons, Howard has helped the Magic build a winning team. He is a team player on both ends of the court. His solid shooting gives the Magic a boost on offense. His excellent rebounding opens up more chances to score. He hopes his skills will lead to an NBA championship someday.

# TIMELINE

1985—Dwight Howard is born December 8 in Atlanta, Georgia.

1998—Howard enrolls at Southwest Atlanta Christian Academy.

2004—Howard wins many national awards; he is drafted by the Orlando Magic in the first round.

2005—Howard becomes the youngest player to score at least 20 points and grab 20 rebounds in one game; he is named to the NBA All-Rookie team.

2007—Howard is named to the NBA All-Star Team.

2008—Howard wins a gold medal with the U.S. Olympic Basketball Team.

2009—Howard leads the Magic to the NBA Finals; he is the youngest player to win the NBA Defensive Player of the Year Award.

# GLOSSARY

**average** (AV-uh-rij)—to find the typical number of points scored or rebounds grabbed in each game

**board** (BORD)—a rebound in basketball

**center** (SEN-tur)—a basketball player who usually plays near the basket and is often the tallest player on the team

**defender** (di-FEN-duhr)—a player who tries to keep the other team from scoring

**draft** (DRAFT)—the process of choosing a person to join a sports team

**rebound** (REE-bound)—the act of gaining possession of the ball after a missed shot

# READ MORE

**Fawaz, John.** *Dwight Howard*. New York: Scholastic, Inc., 2010.

**Harasymiw, Malcolm J.** *Dwight Howard: Superman of Basketball*. Inspiring Lives. New York: Gareth Stevens Pub., 2010.

# INTERNET SITES

FactHound offers a safe, fun way to find Internet sites related to this book. All of the sites on FactHound have been researched by our staff.

Here's all you do:

Visit *www.facthound.com*

Type in this code: 9781429665636

 Check out projects, games and lots more at
**www.capstonekids.com**

# INDEX